Caretakers of Wonder

A Star & Elephant Book
by Cooper Edens

Paper bound ISBN 0-914676-76-8
Hard bound ISBN 0-914676-78-4

A Star & Elephant Book from
The Green Tiger Press

La Jolla, California 92038

This very night,
while you lie quietly in your bed,
open your eyes.
Now, look out your window!
For even at this yawning hour,
so many of your friends
are working to keep
the world magical.

Yes, they are the ones
who make new stars
and put them up.

The ones who light
and keep the stars burning.

The ones who keep the moon company,
feeding him when he's too thin
and watching his diet
when he's too full.

The ones who keep
the sky and the horizon
tightly fastened to each other.

The ones who make sure
that the night
is kept buttoned-up
against the cold.

And do you know
what else is happening?
Yes, even now
some of your friends
are busy making sure
that all is ready
for morning...

They are the ones
weaving the meadows
and telling the trees
where to stand.

The ones putting fruit
back on the branches.

The ones painting
feathers on birds
and
designs on the wings
of butterflies.

The ones practicing
the great rainbow
balancing act.

The ones collecting
yesterday's raindrops,
mending old clouds,
and delivering
newly stuffed ones.

And yes,
all day tomorrow
your friends will be at work
(behind the scenes, of course)...

They are the ones
who will raise the sun
into place.

The ones who will
load up the night
and bring it back
to storage.

The ones who will
give the wind directions,
fly the clouds,
and tell
the rain where to fall.

The ones who will
make changes in the weather
and decide the season.

The ones who will
make sure that the sun
gets down safely.

Now, while you sleep tonight...

...imagine what you most
would like to do
to help keep the world
magical?
For you know
that one of these nights
your friends are going to tap
on your window
and invite you to become
one of the
Caretakers of Wonder.

Color Separation by
Photoprep, San Diego, California and
Ed Marquand/Scanner Graphics, Seattle, Washington

The text in this book was set in Della Robia
by Spartan Typographers, Oakland, California